Also by Dolly Dennis

Loddy-Dah

Guernica Editions, 2014

The Complex Arms

Dundurn Press, 2020

THE QUIET WOUND

The Quiet Wound
Copyright 2025 by Dolly Dennis

This book was independently published by Jane Hikel.
Contact: JaneHikel@yahoo.com

Cover art by Dolly Dennis
Cover design by the LMPatarini group

PAPERBACK ISBN: 979-8-9884171-4-9

THE QUIET WOUND – DOLLY DENNIS

I buried the girl I had been because she ran into all kinds of trouble. I tried to erase every memory of her, but she is still there, somewhere. She is still small and scared and ashamed, and perhaps I am writing my way back to her, trying to tell her everything she needs to hear.

-Roxane Gay, Hunger: A Memoir of (My) Body

CONTENTS

THE QUIET WOUND – DOLLY DENNIS

INTRODUCTION:

SOME THINGS ARE BEST SAID IN A POEM

I have struggled to write this book since I was a teenager. First as therapy to make me feel whole again, civilized, and, secondly, to let others, especially immigrant daughters, understand that it is important to share your experiences of abuse in all its forms even though you may be ignored or discredited. Know that there will always be someone to take your hand, ie, a neighbour, a teacher, a friend, a cop, or a discovered talent, to give you the courage and support to endure, to survive. Mine was painting and writing. That is why this memoir includes some of my early poems and drawings. It all began this way...

After WW2, my family became Lithuanian war refugees, displaced persons, dps or perkeltieji asmenys, a people without a home. The communists ruled Lithuania so my parents could not, would not, return to their homeland. They were stateless. Through sponsorship, we arrived by boat to Canada, February 1952. I was not yet 5. We were forbidden entry into my parents' first choice, the United States of America, the Promised Land, because of my father's dealings in the Black Market during the war.

There have been many books written about the refugee experience and the tenacity of a people whose homes were destroyed or conquered by an enemy. However, The Quiet Wound gives witness to my early memories growing up in a violent household that resulted in feelings of self-rejection, self-criticism, depression, anxiety and, finally, anger. The cruelty of racism, molestation, and poverty has no colour, gender or status. It followed me into the snow banks and muddy ditches of this new place called Montreal, Quebec. I cowered in corners, playgrounds and sheds like an abandoned pup, left to fend for itself. With determination, persistence, and perseverance, I somehow managed to find my road to some form of happiness, to self-love. So here I am, in my greying years, sharing my story, and perhaps it will bring hope and encouragement to those who have also had abuse issues, and have yet to stand up strong and shout: you can't do this to me!

***

In the writing, I've used some Lithuanian vocabulary because I liked their sound, and to convey the sense of the language spoken at home. I have also used some French terms, expletives, to express anger because those were lexemes I heard as a little girl playing in the streets and laneways of Ville Emard and then Verdun, both working class boroughs of Montreal. The phrase Tikras Tevas (just like your father) was constantly hurled at me so I repeat the attack here as an example of hurtful slurs. How does it feel? Soundless. No strap, just cruel words. I realized some things were best said in a poem so this memoir is written in a hybrid format, viewed through the lens of my poetry, prose, captured dialogue, paintings and sketches that guided me to write about the familial violence—physical, mental, emotional, and sexual, which I carried into adulthood. The mental assaults were the most difficult and lasted the longest. Those scars still remain and continue to linger even now as I write this.

***

The Quiet Wound is based on diary entries, which I started to pen as a thirteen-year-old, sitting on the back gallery of our tenement in Verdun. With the invention of the computer, I later printed out the correspondence between my brother and myself, between my best friend, Jane, and my school chum, Gayle, who were like sisters to me. Both were my greatest allies. I believe that because of them, I stayed the course instead of wandering into a path I was accused of treading, ie, a juvenile delinquent, whore, slut, talentless—a nothing. They assured me there was a better world out there than the one I knew. I filed my diary entries into a three-inch thick red folder that I reference here—the facts and nothing but the facts, so help me God. Still I agonized over writing The Quiet Wound and sending it out into the world. I did not yet have the moxie. Would anyone believe me? Would this memoir help someone?

It wasn't until I chanced upon an interview on social media with my little brother, a semi-recognized Canadian poet, where I was mentioned. His lies angered me but also motivated me to speak out, set the record straight. The cyber space attack chapter is an actual transcript of the conversation between us with no editing.

I still did not have the guts to pen into words what had happened to me so I consulted a friend who taught "writing the memoir" and she answered my questions. She explained that I had the right to tell my story, and my brother could write his. I do not name him. Estranged for thirty years, we have deleted each other from existence and his whereabouts are unknown. My divorced parents had long passed into a happier state—I hope! Are there any "normal" families out there? I am reminded of Leo Tolstoy's quote that all happy families are alike; each unhappy family is unhappy in its own way. The Quiet Wound captures the trauma that was my family.

***

I finally reclaimed my voice in this last chapter of my life, and promised that determined girl, growing up on the seedy side of Montreal's immigrant population, to never abandon her, to never disappoint her, to always stand strong, to remind her she has value. My friends jogged my mind for details, filling in the forgotten spaces, which had floated away like driftwood into a sea of memory cells buried deep into the hippocampus as Christine Ford had mentioned at the Kavanagh hearings. I did not want this book to be a he said/she said revenge against my disturbed family, especially my brother, whom I gather, resides somewhere in "Neverland", and continues to be blinded by his victimized narcissism.

The manuscript for The Quiet Wound sat gathering cobwebs for thirty-five years until I blew the dust off the archival cover, the red folder, convinced that this displaced, misplaced girl will be an example for all women, young and old, who have been unspeakably violated. They are not alone. #MeToo. Remember? Raise your arms high, please, alongside mine. A standing ovation deserved for all escapees.

VILLE EMARD

(1952-1957)

BUK ATSARGAS: BE CAREFUL (January 9, 1952)

i am four.

waves of whales, starboard side,

swagger, undulate, procrastinate,

penetrate the ocean floor.

mother vomits,

curses her bad luck.

the *Fairsea* parks at Pier 21,

human cargo from a brutal war—

2

a steady stream of displaced persons, dp's

surge the inclined plank. Lietuviškai kalba—

 Lithuanian spoken here.

toddler feet a stumbling dance,

tumbling to a Welk of polkas.

mother screams Dali, Dali,

frail son at her breast

buk atsargus; be careful;

18

THE QUIET WOUND – DOLLY DENNIS

father flirts with every skirt on deck.

we board the train à Montréal.

sponsors have secured a berth,

a lower flat in Ville Emard—

6427 Briand Street.

folks cavort on shipping crates,

slugging vodka, slurring songs

about the motherland, about the

roadside crosses marking graves

left behind. they sing to forget;

they sing to live. What else to do?

someone plays the akordeona;*

another plucks a stringy kankle,**

stolen instruments snuck on board.

the heels of my tattered shoes drum

against the wooden trunk,

lives jammed into shopping bags of hope,

drunken dreams yet to reap.

mother's wrapped me in a thin wool coat—

a benefactor's gift;

she's thrown me out into the snow,

white hills. left me there to sort my life—

this disposable daughter. sinking, drowning

in an avalanche of tears.

*akordeona— an accordian   ** kankle —string instrument played by

plucking the strings

DETERMINATION

see, how she walks with such determination;

look, how she sings with such resolution

lyrics to *how much is that doggie in the window*

waltzing to the *Tennessee Waltz.*

she will one day trade the words,

write of pain that sears her soul,

a hot iron. she has yet to find

that love can be capricious,

that wounded birds cannot fly

until they are healed.

LITTLE LULA (circa 1952)

dawn ebbs in pink tides of waking up,

my little brother and i, noses pressed against the

bedroom window. mother on the night shift—

assembly line of refugees packing bread.

Ogilvy Flour Mills, an English establishment

will speed up the conveyor belt—

>   until she drops.

no like émmigranté she will later say,

her young hands knarled in white dough.

our father has gone missing,

unemployable; all jobs below his rank—

>   this medical student from Lithuania.

i am in charge.

little brother has looted mother's nail polish.

pink like morning light.

paints a canvas,

squiggles on the pane—

      hieroglyphics in a toddler's scrawl.

he is three.

in later years he will define himself a poet,

a genius writing at an early age,

inventing language on a window of pain—

      he will strip my soul.

and here she comes.

cuts the corner from the bus stop, Monk onto Briand,

through Garneau Park, a time saver;

head down against the wind, packages under wrap,

gloveless; drops her bags in a rush of hugs and kisses—

      revealing sweets and Baltic bread.

brought us comics: Little Lulu for me; Bugs Bunny for him.

no books insulate our home. i will learn to

read next year at Holy Cross, fall in love

with the scent and sound of pages turning.

but for now—

Little Lulu is my friend.

LITTLE GIRL SINGS THE BLUES (for Patti Page, 1955)

this backyard is a stage of cracked clay.

nothing grows here; not even children.

     i buy *The Hit Parader* and *Song Hits,*

learn the lyrics to the *Billboard* sounds of Patti Page and Gale Storm,

collect the latest *Movie Screen* and *Photoplay,*

conceal the mags behind the bedroom door.

tievas* finds the hiding place,

my secret life oozes out—

a rage of madness flows; red hot lava burns my dreams.

     i am in Old Cape Cod.

not here, this swamp called home,

full throttle straight ahead

     submerge the slaps and screams,

beats me good, cussing my existence.

Patti Page sings of sand dunes and salty air.

my arms reach out, an audience of clouds applaud me.

the leather belt doesn't hurt.

again.

*tievas — father

INVISIBLE REFUGEE

i am lily white—

icing sugar, a displaced person, an unmasked refugee,

an orphan with a mother and a father but no country.

no hijab, niqab to conceal my face, reveal my faith.

Saturday classes in the church cellar calcify my culture;

lest i forget the words: labas—hello. su dievu—goodbye.

Lithuanian folk costumes—

girls dance, flounce in an embroidery of apron skirts

bounce to every kick of the legs.

a coronet in yellow, green and red ribbons, colours of the

homeland flag, crown the head like a tiara; boys sashay in sashes,

shirts with billowy sleeves, harem trousers fan the air;

scarlet boots slick like chapstick polish off the ethnic look.

ridiculed by mis-pronunciations—

we anglicize our names. remain silent until coerced to speak and then the secret: we are invisible refugees.

my name devours half the alphabet—

Danguoli Benedicta Filipavicius but who would remember or even

care?

mother calls me Dali; the neighbour upstairs

registers me for school as Dolly. Close enough.

                              a rejected summer job—

Zellers won't hire; too foreign a name.

should have changed to Dahlia, the flower of elegance and dignity

or just say my name Dolly as in hello.

                              empty kitchen cupboards—

a daily dose of Mazola, sustenance until the vulture gains employment.

i hide in dusty laneways, sit on strangers' doorsteps,

wait for mama to return from a factory of hell.

neighbours take me in, feed this miserable waif, i become

an extra chair, learn to swear in foreign tongues—

English, Polish, French, Lithuanian, some Italian.

an invisible refugee—

i wear pigtails, climb 'phone poles, scamper on rooftop sheds, disturb

rats,

both the vermin and the human kind; steal lipstick from the five and

dime;

pick apples from Italian gardens; hunger for unlimited love and peace,

a touch of courage, nothing more for this expendable daughter, sister.

a child tossed in a winter sink hole, a snow bank; no trace of her

whereabouts.

WHIPLASH

a plumbic sky—

overstayed my visit in the sandbox,

missed my bath, busy building castles.

mother drags me home,

hauls me into the tub,

father drifts above,

devil incarnate,

knotted clothesline in his clutch,

no where else to go.

the first whiplash—

a gasp for air;

the second—

rips my toddler's back;

submerging in a rash of red,

water on skin, skin on water,

a searing slash. the red sea

splashes in a scalding dunk.

LET HER BE!

      the third—

bruises mother's legs, bare as bone.

her breasts leaning forward,

lifts me up up up.

      the fourth—

      strikes us both.

SCENES FROM A CHILDHOOD

take 1:

six years old.

i play hide and seek. scrunch myself into an empty crate of mandarins,

cache in Primo's shed among the rice and mice.

Fury tagged me, tickled my sweet nose, arms, and cheeks.

he is twelve.

i giggled as little girls are apt to do; slid my panties to my knees;

placed his ear against my groin. What's he listening for?

touched my girlhood like a whisper,

lips and fingers brushed his hands against its smallness.

take 2:

eight years old.

awakened by a full moon.

an animal in distress. someone left the TV on.

closed my eyes but still...a ruckus in the cellar.

went to see.

mother's skirt gathered, knotted above her head

like an overturned umbrella in a gust of wind,

cold-cocked, she laid stock-still. when done

he yelped like a dog; collapsed in exhaustion.

she thrashed about drowning in the cell of bedding.

take 3:

ten years old.

home from school.

photo on the kitchen table,

the vulture and his two naked sluts

smiling like a picnic on a sunny day.

take 4:

twelve years old.

a foreign car parked in the old carriage lane,

just appeared. no food in the fridge but we have wheels.

children tramped, jumped on its roof like a trampoline.

dents and bents and scents of gas,

he appeared and scolded them—

hai hai hai. the kids retorted in their bad French:

maudit cochon polack pig, damn immigrant.

i sit here trembling with memory.

VERDUN

(1958-1969)

THE HOUSE ON EVELYN STREET

we are moving on

down

down

down

drowning in my father's shit,

trading one slum for another,

East Verdun, neighbour to the Pointe,

a depanneur on every corner,

beer and chips on demand.

the landlord lives below; a tenant upstairs in the front,

and we, the three of us, in back, animals in a cage—

one bedroom, living room, kitchen, covered porch,

shared bathroom, fissure in the door jamb,

 a slight light escapes.

i am standing in the tub, acting in the mirror

Marilyn in *Something's Got to Give*.

the hallway floor squeaks, an eyeball

for an eyeball. mine and his.

a flutter of angel wings, a tramp of lion paws,

a flurry of steps hurry, scurry

down

down

down.

his door clicks like a sleepy infant.

i tell no one. next time i thread a facecloth

through the peeping hole; bathe in darkness,

shiver at the flashback. forget to breathe.

CORNER OF VERDUN AND HICKSON
(for Gayle)

knee deep in December, Christmas a week away, my skates a hanging,

a dangling tangle of shoelaces when he interrupts my flight—

where you going? i know you're meeting men. no pa, says i. *i'm*

meeting a friend and she's waiting at the bus stop and i'll be late and

she'll be mad and i have to just go. just go. he sliced open a brown

paper lunch bag with a flick of his dime store pocket knife; laid it flat

like a new hankie; ordered me to map my route. the X's marked the

bus stops; the lines measured streets and avenues; the O stood for the

skating rink. a catawampus of nervous directions to St. Willibrord

park. a game of X O X with me the loser, an extra X pending, fits here

now, the unknown factor. the beast scrunched the paper in a wad of

cruelty and pitched it like a runaway baseball towards my head. *said*

you're staying put. i pleaded, choked back words, on the brink of

fainting. *let me at least meet my friend, tell her i can't go. she'll be*

freezing from the wait. the creep remained immune to my silent tears;

the world slipped off its axis. then without a thought he slowly

snapped his eyelids open like an owl waking up; *go quick and come*

41

back quicker or you'll get your you know whats. i knew the whats and

so my short teenage legs flittered like a hummingbird numb to the

gelid winter threat.

*****

an opaque darkness. Verdun avenue; you standing at the corner bus

stop fuming, rime on your tuque and scarf, stomping your feet to keep

warm, a face red as ripe tomatoes. *'bout time!* you scolded as the wind

guided me across the street before the light switched colour. a squeal

of brakes, *kill me kill me,* my silent prayer as i skated on road ice. a

bus careened to a halt. i vanished in your arms. *wanna get killed girl?*

the driver screamed. *yes, please,* i whispered as though ordering a root

beer. *i can't go, i can't go* and your anger changed to worry as you

lifted me up, flakes of tears and tumbling snow sifting underneath the

streetlight as the bus drove off without us. you knew but what could

you do?

*****

when i reached home, he attacked with vile profanities. groping hands

smacked my face, my breasts; grabbed my groin. i had learned to

ignore the pain. *whore tramp kurva, like your mother.* he smashed my

42

soul against the fridge pummelling me with his masochistic pleasure, his noxious body a battering ram of fat, bone and booze. i bounced from wall-to-wall in a game of catch me if you can. my spirit surfed towards the open door. mother, an apparition in winter wool, poised in the doorway, recoiled, evacuated like a house on fire, her customary mantra jesu jesu dragged behind until only my mumbled confession echoed into the pavement. a dead end. his demonic laugh haunts me to this day.

*****

remember slummy Verdun, Gayle? it's become gentrified "prettified"—converted condos stand where once a squalour of broken-down tenements and tenants quenched dignity; a scatter of outdoor "chi-chi" patios now dot Wellington, the place to break bagels and eat poutine, squander a day's pay on beer; a fake beach behind the auditorium where once we heard Gerry and the Pacemakers sing *Ferry Cross the Mersey*. now gone. all gone. we were such groupies you and i. you should see how Montreal has re-invented itself. French signs re-write history, scars persist. dried-up political scabs dot the city's skin.

Leonard Cohen, in a welcome mural, overlooks our playground,

Crescent Street, defying separatists to deface his poetic presence.

*****

i no longer live there, Gayle. the day i launched my first book, a sour

skyline like only Montreal could muster circled the Hotel 10. i met

your cousin and goddaughter, executors of your estate. an awkward

moment, they reached out to me, presenting a small silver box. *she*

would have wanted you to have this. it had been pouring all day, a

reoccurring melancholy of nails hammering the wet sidewalks, rue

Sherbrooke, and the Main. i just wanted you here. you were supposed

to wait for me. we were like sisters even though we differed on so

many counts. you and your parents taught me how to seek a better life

and not give up too soon on my dreams. i didn't. when i praised my

brother's status, an award-winning published poet, you hushed me up

and insisted on hearing about the book i was writing. so here i am.

your goddaughter placed the box in my hand and said, *it's her baby*

ring. i glanced out the picturesque front window of the hotel lobby,

and i swear the sun vibrated, announced its presence for a minute, or

was that you knocking in a thunderbolt? *i've come to hear you read,* you said. i caught your contagious baby giggle, felt your protective

arms like on that winter day when you waited for me at the bus stop,

lifting up my spirit so many years ago.

*****

as suddenly as the sun appeared, it disappeared behind a shroud of

angry clouds and the sky resumed its life. a busted pipe or perhaps

someone up there had left the water running, backing up the sewers.

was that you Gayle? you and your naughty hijinks.

A TOMATO MESS

he was leaving for work.

night was the start of his day.

little brother and i cowered on the lip of fear.

a skirmish at the front door: he was assaulting

her and this time i called the cops.

he's killing her he's killing her come quick.

he halted in a rage of sweat and hurled his

paper lunch bag at the living room wall.

an explosion, juice dripping like a bloody Pollock

pour. a tomato mess.

he was about to break her jaw but i got in the way,

a boulder between them. where did i get such sass?

don't you dare hit my mother. don't you fuckin' dare.

his hand flew towards my face, froze in mid-air.

startled at my impudence, he remained speechless.

no one had ever resisted, tested, this predator.

i braced for a beating; instead he made a 'u-ey'.

bolted down the stairs like the lone ranger.

the next night we fled; MIA displaced persons #2

escaping under a temper tantrum of horizontal raindrops slapping,

stabbing at our backs, worldly goods filled in two shopping bags.

a stolen Steinberg's cart propelled us forward.

and fear.

no turning back. death was the trade off.

the moonless night hid our tracks.

trudging five blocks to a new three-storey walk-up.

moving on up up up. barely. closer to the rainbow.

seventeen. a graduate from the Motherhouse,

i learned to type. hired on in a steno pool of hope.

there was my income after all, always my income defined me.

i was good for something. a new life on third avenue.

KNIT DRESSES

she knits

      until her wrists drop numb—

a girlhood dress in autumn red,

a dropped stitch, picked up here and there,

      knit purl

      purl knit,

repeat first row

      purl purl;

a click of speeding needles:

      repeat repeat to end of row.

      bind off.

i spin

      around the kitchen floor—

Baryshnikov in mid-air, round and round,

a flying saucer dressed in virgin wool,

exposing ruby lacey panties.

later

      she will knit me sheaths—

form-fitting dresses worn to church

hugging teenage hips and breasts,

a leather belt cinched around my tiny waist.

you

      will snap photos—

mother waving in a field of dandelions gone to seed,

a Jackie Kennedy wannabe suited in bouffant pink.

me

      in long white gloves—

posing on a slope of grass and weed,

the church behind. Aušru Varta, Lady Gate of Dawn.

      Lithuanian   sex   symbol.

after all the cruel words, lies—

      we turned our backs on one another,

a brother and a sister, alienated strangers to the end.

you

      confessed to an erection

ogling me do Marilyn in a dresser mirror,

THE QUIET WOUND – DOLLY DENNIS

smeared my name, trilingual slurs—

    slut *kurva **putain.

    my fault, you said.

    i didn't know—

    i just wanted to dance.

*kurva — slut in Lithuanian

**putain — slut in French

PORTRAIT OF THE ARTIST
IN HER PUSSYCAT HAT

the sofa bed belonged to me

and baby brother—

until that night.

a vulture gnawed my private parts,

attacked the soft tissues first,

clawed up my chest between my breasts,

pulled at my nipples; stiff like fear,

his mouth wide-open in an oh ho ho,

tongue flicking, licking

back and forth

back and forth

and then he stopped.

i will teach you how to love said the predator

no man can hurt my little girl.

and mother standing in the doorway

wailing

jesu, jesu, jesu.

this puling preteen, innocence ruptured

interrupted beyond repair. no fairy tale.

a sudden thrust in messy sheets; red ink sputters

down my thigh and she is gone with utters of

      jesu jesu jesu.

returns with a tampon, a rampant rocket launches in my face.

i won't do it again, i won't. i promise.

      what does a child understand?

that she was touched where no man had a right to go;

that no one would believe, not even her mama

who bore witness. *i don't want to talk* she said.

next day on her way to church

      jesu, jesu, jesu tagged along.

jesus had nothing to do with it.

      after a thousand yesteryears

outracing insults and assaults,

my fingers drilled through a lambent,

a black hole where new universes birth,

stitched me back to life,

  a damaged daughter, a frayed rag doll,

 surfacing in a parade of pink pussy cat hats,

a stretch of arms reach to the sky.

  *#MeToo#MeToo#MeToo.

*a women's movement

WRITING ON THE GREY BACK PORCH

a million black birds,

i swear,

spill out

and mob the summer sky,

a bas relief of wings.

Night.

YEARLING

the house sparrow

with the broken wing writhes side-to-side,

sweeps the backyard lane with injured plumes.

such moxie for a yearling, yearning, learning how to fly.

the frantic mother bird

chirps from a hidden nest: *buck up buck up buck up.*

the epileptic fledging seizes with such horror; still alive,

thrashes to the song *i'm like a bird*, sung from a radio

nearby. *fuck up fuck up fuck up* the father bird caws with lust.

the sparrow struggles

with a stubborn streak. such tenacity, such audacity,

arms swinging in tandem to its speeding heartbeat,

still a yearling healing every day

leaning forward, parachute in place. one day

she will zoom between the rows of

clouds,

surf a rainbow, touch down in a field of prairie grass, a euphoric high

minus drugs; ready for her closeup Mr. Cecil B. De Mille,

a Hollywood ending—

a star in the making.

MY ROOM

                        i am banished, exiled,

confined to the enclosed back porch, a cubby hole

the dimensions of a walk-in closet

a prison in *Paynes Grey,*

my rolled-up cot abuts the shed; an apple crate,

my nightstand, sports a sculptured bear in clay.

                        i paint immeasurable dreamscapes,

the immensity of the universe.

the walls have inherited my art,

a bid to blot out bitter cracks. i pick at scabs.

a parched parrot etched in blond plywood, 9 x 12,

broods on a limb in Van Gogh hues of blue and

red and hooker green.

a sketch of JFK above my bed,

pasted on purple paper, ignites my grief,

burns like an eternal flame.

in memoriam. to me.

who did that says my mama.

i did.

you lie.

my art teacher says i can draw.

your art teacher know nothing.

i only know this isolation; how winter

solidifies the snow into ice; converts into melt water in spring.

fabricated walls without insulation in the fall; the chilly

leakage of air preserves my lungs. the sundog dormant

on the carpet without hue, no halos to excite the day.

i have learned to love winter; to search for the northern lights.

beyond my prison walls, a portal

leads to the kitchenette. a muffled noise of slaps escape

into a pack of smacks, ugliness seeping beneath the closed door.

a feral shriek. i am awake. race toward the screams.

he is there convulsing on the floor in periods of four jazz beats,

his head a target for his gun; mother watching,

mummified with a short attention span of sobs.

she is programmed to call on jesu jesu jesu.

he never comes. a squeal of sirens brakes in front.

MELANCHOLIA IN THE KEY OF FAURE

fallen apples on the orchard floor grieve the day—

a hill of red and brown sluice a trampled path,

wounded fruit among the dead dry leaves;

pallid hands dig and dig

shove the dirt away,

reveal a rustic road.

a tornado of leaves buries me—

the wind betrays.

a requiem for loss.

give me a moment,

let me grip my heart.

grasp its prize.

i stab a hand through muddy castles,

soak arthritic hands in solstice suds.

le soleil

sauli

the sun.

A QUIET WOUND

"Unlike wounds resulting from physical or sexual abuse,
where the invasive energy is blatant, the wounding energy
of emotional incest is stealthy and very difficult to track and
therefore heal."   *...Paul Dunion, EdD*

the weary night in full denial drapes the moon early;

autumn's shadows stretch lank and threatening.

i shield myself in a fort of magazines,

transport dreams to a land of la la la,

sleep and sleep, the sleep of movie stars.

father heaves the pulpy mags into the trash;

a vomit of curses follow spitting venom.

i enfold into an origami. a still life. i watch

him pulverize my Movie Screens and Photoplays,

kami paper paints my pain, a quiet wound

not displayed, unable to heal. only silent anger remains.

WEATHER REPORT

to this day i cannot tolerate the sweaty tropics;

instead, i choose to walk shoeless on scenic icefields,

seek the path least trampled leading to the north

where darkness draws the land early,

where moody clouds meet the mountain snow.

exposed feet dangle out the thermal covers—

liberation from the oppressive heat of living.

SOUND OF SHOVELLING SNOW

how to explain the sound of cold?

it's buried under hills of snow; gesso on an artist's palette

surprises like a *jack-in-the-box*, assaults the city overnight

declaring war. holds winter victims hostage.

pick your weapon: shovels, blowers, brooms.

and then it hits me—

how the snow insulates the day,

blows blind; blizzards coat deserted streets

conceal the unattended laneways.

listen to the muffled voices—

snow speaks slow, a vocabulary all its own.

we got a dump last night, aye.

i can't hear from the shovelling.

the skid of tires squeal, break the windrows

of my mind; the scratch of scraping windshields,

chalk on blackboards, brittle frozen jitters.

a garbled cough; the fresh crinkle of saran wrap,

vapourizes, crystalizes into ice.

      a mural of frost on the screen door window.

stubby thumbnails carve my name—

i slip inside; lock the door behind,

first sip of the day warms my voice.

coffee perking; the strain of winter waking.

MOVIELAND

i want to be

Sandra Dee

Gidget on a surfboard machine

anyone

but me.

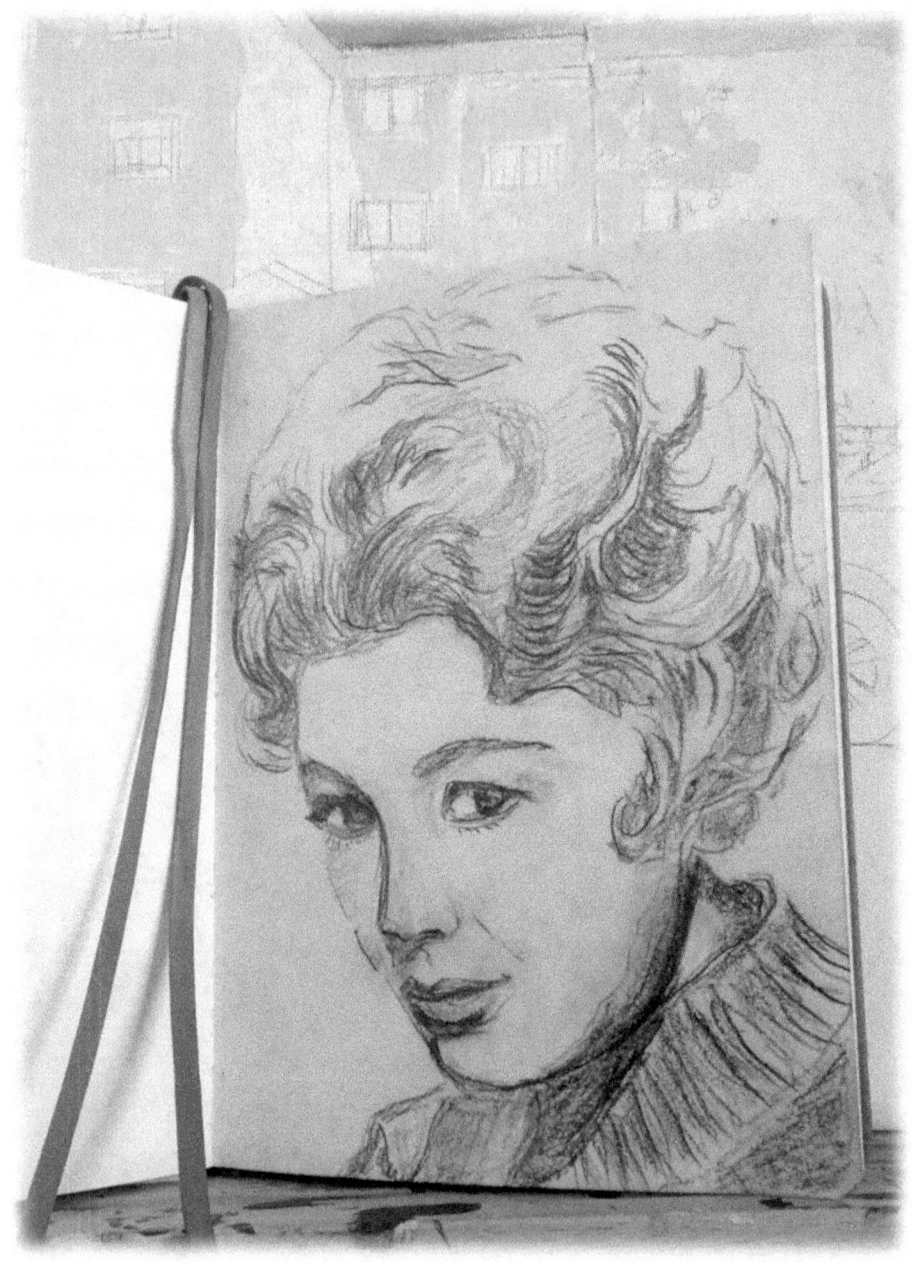

ONE PIZZA PLEASE *(Third Avenue 1965)*

What I remember about your moving away from Evelyn St. is that you were the one who made the move and that you told your mother, "I have the apartment and you can come with me or stay, but I'm going". I thought you were incredibly independent and strong. I remember visiting you and there was a phone call. The number had previously been assigned to a takeout restaurant. I hear you say, yes, one pizza, ok, bye. That was so funny. We laughed about the people waiting for their pizza to arrive. You said, eventually, they will realize that this is not the pizza restaurant.

...Jane, my best friend forever

WINDY SUNFLOWERS (for Van Gogh)

sunflowers make me weep —

those giant clod-hoppers undulate

fornicate the breeze. no wonder

Van Gogh painted them.

stubborn, leggy, robust

acned faces scarred and charred

hair ablaze, a golden beacon

for the castaways, rejected squatters

tagged as weeds.

sunflowers carry madness —

such a burden for so bright a bloom.

muddy back yards, bare and barred,

weary heads droop and scoop,

genuflect the garden floor.

cockeyed bonnets all askew

petals slanted in a tilt of plates

scatter like a wedding day.

littered dreams buried deep.

"When I entered the hall, I felt like saying, 'Take off your shoes, for the place where you are standing is Holy Ground"...Van Gogh upon entering a hall selling drawings by his hero, Jean-Francois Millet.

MESSAGE FROM VAN GOGH

and he my hero

stood beside me, earless, fearless.

cupped his mouth and whispered—

you'll be fine.

use your talents dearest one.

be brave, dare

and i will send you starry nights.

your friend,

Vincent

BELIEVE HER

Thanks for filling me in on the abuses you underwent. I knew about your father as I very well remember the time you told me what was going on. I think we were in high school and you were living on Evelyn Street. We had gone to a concert or something and it was late and you told me that I could sleep over at your place. I think we were already asleep on the couch, I believe. Your mother and brother were sleeping in the bedroom, which I found very strange. Your father came home and he may have been drunk. He was yelling at us that he did not want that going on in his house. I think he was accusing us of being lesbians, now that I think about it. Sometime later, you told me that he had been abusing you and your mother was allowing it to happen. She had to have been aware. I remember thinking after you told me about him that it was probably why he did not want me to be there. That was horrible for you. I did not know that you had those abusive and violent experiences once you were living on your own, and my heart goes out to you. I wish there was something I could have done. I am grateful that you ended up with a good man.

Your experience shows that women don't talk about these traumas until years later, not even sharing them with their best friends. Even though I never had anything as horrific happen to me, I felt shame and humiliation when some stranger touched me inappropriately (once it was an eye doctor while my mother was sitting right across the room). You never forget these things. That is why I say, believe her.

It is painful for you to be writing this book, but it is a good thing you are doing. Wish I could give you a hug to keep you going. Just know that I am with you and if there is anything I can do to help, all you have to do is ask.

Love,

Jane, your best friend forever

FOR MY PAPA WHO WASN'T VERY WONDERFUL

you sitting

at the kitchen table carrying the weight of

the world, the thinker. bloody facial gashes,

see what they do. your folded blood-stained clothes

a heap of rags, the place we eat, now reeks of shit and

spit on this muggy summer day. reckless driver;

speeding foreign car smashed beyond repair but you survived.

see what they do. see what they do. tears shimmered down

the bloodied wrinkles of your unshaved face.

what did

they do? what did they do to conceive such madness?

such sadness beyond repair. don't blame the war,

or a loveless marriage, laziness perhaps.

other refugees have endured your prison term,

arrived, survived, thrived. beatified Canada, blessed this country,

but you. what did they do to create this madman?

my birth

pre-dates your wedding. occupation: medicus studentus,

a big shot nothing dabbling in the black market in Kiel.

you denied paternity. fake papers justified the evil done

to me and mamamyte*? *don't want to talk;* she never does.

whom do I believe? Mary Magdalena or the devil?

you built

a fence between your own mama and sister,

abandoned them in Lithuania, denied their existence.

as my brother will deny mine. what was done to you

to breed such hate? such contempt? such animosity?

i am an orphan you said. i have no ties to a family.

one day

i caught you doodling on the table; the blood-stained clothes had dried.

you smirked and flung the sketch at me. *see what i can do.*

scribbled cartoons on the margins of a life.

77

is this what the medical student can do?

war interrupted your plans, the burden of a deformed son,

a moody daughter and a factory wife erased your dream.

you now patrol the harbour front, a uniformed guard in Pinkerton blue,

spraying graffiti on sheds and sides of ships, leaving fingerprints—

i was here you scrawled in broken English; no other skills need apply.

*Mamamyte — endearment for mother.

FINAL TEASE (1968, Verdun, Quebec)

brought to my knees,

corner of Wellington and De l'église.

sightless from the burning light, a cataract figure

in a puddle of sun; a security guard securing no one.

unrecognizable. dressed in Pinkerton blue.

an endurance of years, waiting for the streetlight to change.

a showdown in a western film,

we drifted toward each other's shadow,

falling kites, strangers now.

a brief intersection.

he, with some perverted pleasure, skims my arm;

me, wounded daughter levitating. tiny follicles prickle,

tickle, electrify the contact. apnea in daylight,

the final rub, the familiar stench of

Vodka, Cigarillo, Old Spice.

we reach our stations,

bases on the street corners. last inning mounting.

THE QUIET WOUND – DOLLY DENNIS

a simultaneous glance over shoulders,

a choreographed dance to acknowledge, recognize,

and then the tease, a rapid release.

i evaporate.

SKETCHING MY MOTHER FROM A PHOTO

you must have loved me once—

i can see how you held me near

a bastard child with a pout

stout like a boulder, an only child

'til my brother came along

and things began to change.

i draw with graphite pencils—

eyes reflect my own

as does the nose,

the rest is his.

i touch the photo,

fingers trace your face and hair,

your mouth.

i would erase your pain if I could,

THE QUIET WOUND – DOLLY DENNIS

instead i tour your life

 and weep for your lost youth,

a Baltic girl chased by war and evil men—

if you had known then

what you know now,

would you have thrown yourself

out a window sooner?

BALTIC BREAD

autumn.

unraked lawns,

yards of lilac twigs garnish gardens, now ignored.

a new school year. i comb neglected leaves,

meditate, salivate, remember black bread and sour cream—

after class, a sprint to the bakery shop.

such a hunger for a six-year-old. i start to nibble,

nosh like Alice down the rabbit hole;

reach home, the heel of the bread gone.

a scolding. no super supper tonight,

no sauerkraut, no Baltic bread.

just sour cream on nothing.

your last words to me from your hospital bed,

i love you, love you, love you.

a profusion, a confusion of phone dates followed—

Dali, no Sunday. you were chomping down your

smashed potatoes in a sauce of ketchup,

so unlike your daily Baltic bread and cepilinai.*

no ma, it's Saturday. a bewilderment of lost time.

i love you, love you, your alto voice

pierced the line from Montreal to Edmonton.

i joined in a duet of love songs,

a mother and a daughter, one last time.

that's why i called a day early. your son's threat

to separate us needed intervention.

did you say it or did he invent the lie—

i never want to see you again. i leave you nothing.

what did i do? exhausted from a pandemic

game of minds that erupted without notice,

you jumped from your second-floor window.

got my attention and now what?

an occasion for your son to revise his tall tale—

a mix-up of meds left your brain cells busy, dizzy, he said.

you had leaned against the unlocked window screen

plunging into an abyss of dead hedges below

short of being stabbed by the wrought iron fence.

which is the truth?

*cepilinai — Zeppelin, (a popular Lithuanian native dish)

EMBROIDERED APRON*   (for my mama)

in our litany of calls over the years, you had warned—

if i call and there's no answer, call your brother.

and so that Saturday, i did. some woman answered,

said she couldn't talk to me or she'd be in trouble—

words of a violated wife. then his voice interrupted:

yeah, she jumped. she didn't want you to know.

i escaped to save myself. didn't want to hurt you all;

it was time for your sweet **sunus to take care of you.

i was tired of the lies, the drama; the assaults; the insults;

tired of accommodating you. tired of living,

tired of the unraked autumn leaves. #tired #tired #tired.

i am sitting on the apex of a rainbow waiting for the love

to slide down and catch me before i hang up the phone.

one more encore in three-part harmony to be sure:

#i love you#i love you#i love you

in case you didn't hear me through the chewing.

*Embroidered Apron — part of Lithuanian costume

**sunus — son

SKETCHING MY FATHER FROM A PHOTO

too painful.

can't.

DEATH OF MY FATHER

the day

you lay dying, mama phoned—

cancer had attacked your throat,

cut out your tongue,

muted your rage.

i didn't attend your funeral. no memorial service.

what was there that was so memorable?

you didn't deserve a daughter's presence.

instead i remained in bed; entered the twilight zone,

drank a bottle of wine to erase the past;

took up my paint brushes and wept—

not for your death but for the loss of my childhood,

for the woman i could have been; for the father you never were.

INTERVIEW: ATTACK OUT OF CYBERSPACE

(Actual transcript of a conversation between my brother and myself. Like a lot of arguments, some things get repeated because one or the other party was not listening.)

* * *

A zero day. The sun has been thunderstruck by amnesia and has forgotten to make an appearance. Already it is the end of August and only wildflowers are revealing their true colours in the farmers' fields and meadows beyond.

I google my name, see what the universe has to say, and there he is—my little brother. A literary magazine is interviewing him about a poem he wrote following the death of our father, my molester. Shredding family secrets into torn pieces of litter, he scatters the lies into the wind, polluting the ecosphere. My initial impulse was to promptly press the delete button, eliminate further damage to my psyche and shut down the computer. But my curiosity carried the day so I joined in his dialogue. At that time, we had not spoken in over twenty years and now here we were. Previous attempts at reconciliation always failed so I had no expectations.

Maya Angelou, writer, poet and civil rights activist said, "when people show themselves the first time, believe them". People do not change. Little brother initially had a tantrum when he realized it was me, and not some adoring literary fan interrupting the on-line chatter. The reporter seemed to be annoyed at first but, nonetheless, she let my brother speak out: *"There you go again, sneaking around...."* What did he mean? What is he afraid of? Another time, I would have hidden in his shadows; muted my own outrage, waited like I always did until he finished cursing me.

Little brother accused me of character assassination in this public domain, the Internet; that I had run and hid, riding on his coattails again. Run? Cyperspace is without borders. Let me excavate his interred memory cells; sort through the malicious personal attacks that would bring me to my knees. I carry journals, notebooks and e-mails, testimony to the facts. My name can be found with a simple search engine. No sneaking around. It is not my style; maybe his. So here I am, little brother, yoo-hoo, shoot me with your best lies.

* * *

ME: Who is the manipulator you ask? Not sure what you mean except that indeed I left no forwarding address because we are estranged; thirty years as of this writing. I feared that your re-entry into my life, with your judgemental smearing tactics, would throw me into a black hole, never to be seen again as was your custom. You could have e-mailed me as in the past but, no, it was to your advantage to call me the devious emotional narcissist to gain sympathy from friends and a handful of social media fans who knew only your public persona. You removed me from your bio in various literary catalogues. I did not exist. Even our parents received a mention in Canadian Literature, *"...his mother cleaned other people's houses while his father worked as a security guard."* Period. Nothing about a sister—author, playwright, poet, actress, visual artist.

Your lies need corrective therapy as you were the one who assassinated my character at every turn of the phrase: I have no sister you said so it is up to me to defend my reputation, and expose the

truth, a term you disliked because you continued to remain delusional

in your tiny kingdom, "Lord of the Quebec Poets." This is my story to

tell. Not yours.

YOU: As your brother, I have always had the impossible task of trying

to protect you from yourself. To understand you better, I studied

research about PIS. To understand mama and papa better, I set foot on

Lithuanian soil. You have stubbornly refused to do both. (Now who is

the manipulator)? That would take courage and integrity. Yet you

pretend to "set the record straight". Your words skip like a broken

record that I have heard too many times.

ME: Who died and designated you Freud. I had never heard the word

PIS until you started to mention it at every short encounter. I looked it

up: post incest syndrome. To understand all of you better, that it

wasn't my fault, that I was the victim, I consulted psychology books

about victimization, about the war. I had no money to set foot on

Lithuanian soil to empathize, sympathize. I didn't need to travel that far to understand your neurosis, your delusions of grandeur, or our father's psychosis.

Did our mother pay your way with the money I gave her for rent when I lived with her? Travelling back to the homeland is not the only means to rationalize our parents and a culture that degraded our mother as worthy enough to sing in the choir every Christmas but not sit in the front pew of the church with all the mink coats. It is unfortunate that you never knew your older sister, a missed opportunity, and that is why I am once again like a broken record repeating myself so that perhaps you would use your fucking airhead for a brain, to let it finally sink in. You were loved by a disturbed father who carried you as a toddler in his arms in the backyard on Evelyn Street, drove you at high speeds along the river in leased foreign cars. You were loved by a mother who blamed herself for your facial paralysis by letting the German doctors remove the birth mark on your right wrist with an experimental white powder that stunted the arm's growth. *You be okay mama told me once but your little brother, he need help.* Not enough love to go around I guess. I loved you anyway because you were family, my little brother.

YOU: Let me point out all the cracks in your broken record:

The sibling rivalry, the "competition" that you talk about, has always come from your side. In the interview on the web, I clearly state: *this is why I don't call myself an artist.* Making music, making a meal, or making a golf swing—they're all just part of daily rhythms. I'm not competing against anyone—just like mama! I have moved on. I'm into golf now, and into maintaining a healthy body and a healthy mind. Something I have encouraged you to do because of your sick, obese body, and mind games.

ME: My pretentious, narcissistic little nothing of a brother. As we used to say, "names will never hurt me." Did you look at the photos I sent you? I'm 18 and playing guitar. Frustrated with only learning chords, I put the guitar down and switched to writing poems which eventually led me to the Revue Theatre. That girl you tossed into the river, mentioned in your poem, was plain, naive, lacking self-confidence, self-worth. The Artistic Director years later, when I asked why he hired me said: *"after reading your poetry manuscript, I saw something—an innovative talent, uniqueness, originality."* I was stunned! Odd that it took a stranger to see my potential, while you, our mother and father did unspeakable damage to that teenage girl who with great fear searched for shadows to be inconspicuous, go unnoticed. I felt my poems were worthless like I was and discovered that was not the case.

You, my little snap of a brother, picked up my guitar and, eventually, after a few lessons, became a proficient guitarist and teacher. Not in the manner of George Harrison but enough to compose noise that you called music, and to write pretentious lyrics with horrendous sound bites. I gave you that and the next thing I knew, you were also writing poetry following in my footsteps again. I didn't want you to feel neglected. You couldn't do anything well. But I always praised and encouraged whatever interests you showed even when I thought your compositions were pompous, constipated nonsense, a newborn trying to let out gas.

BTW glad to hear about your love affair with golf.

I had to be cautious whenever our paths collided, stepping on egg shells around you to avoid your cruel tactics. Why does a brother assail a sister who always protected him and our mother against our father? To raise his own sense of grandeur?

We squabbled over who wrote poetry first. You always invalidated my rhymes to the point where we wrangled over each other's "masterpiece". I was composing love poems to my pre-teen idols—Tony Dow, Frankie Avalon. You jumped one up on me and shouted as loud as your little mouth could holler that at three, you had invented a new cuneiform on the living room window with our mother's nail polish, squiggly worm-like doodles, and nothing more.

You probably don't remember. But I do. I've kept notes. You were an abuser even then (part of your inherited DNA), so I have overlooked your description of my sick obese body and mind games because I never debased myself to your level of stupidity. You exposed one side of your face to invite pity and, on the other side, behind closed doors, revealed your true character. My weight varied through pregnancy and menopause. Hormones wreck havoc on a woman's body. Your depth of malice towards me knew no bounds.

Poor little brother. Ironic how I could have tagged you with many painful descriptions from your disfigurement to your inferior intelligence while growing up, but I had this attribute called compassion, kindness, and love—until now. I have my limits. Sadism was, and still is, your middle name—always seeking your fifteen minutes of fame in an ancestral land, Lietuva, that did not even recognize you. You are no hero. You are a legend in your own mind. I loved you and understood our mother's devotion to you. A mother's guilt. I was blind to your deformities, mutilation of a hand in Lubeck by the doctors in the dp camp, leaving one limb shorter than the other, a broken wing. I always saw you whole and treated you as such, a little brother latching on to his big sister for a lifeline. But that was not enough. Did you want my sympathy too? Mama asked me when was it that we no longer loved each other. We used to get along. *"Love your brother,"* she would say.

I left the poetry to you and became a playwright. My first effort won two awards at the Quebec Drama Festival. That was in the 70s. You came to see *The Plexiglass Box* at the Revue Theatre where it ran for two weeks. I still carry this image of you bouncing with a jauntiness bordering on relief and arrogance as we left for Ben's Deli

after the show. We had sold out! But you, you spoiled it for me, said

what a disappointment the play was. What a disappointment I was.

That hurt. Emotional abuse. A quiet wound.

Years later when we were in one of our communicative phases,

I announced my pregnancy and you countered that your latest

girlfriend thought she was pregnant. And our mother saying to me *"Oh*

shit!" as though I were a whore. No congratulations or excitement like

most decent families would offer. I was married after all. Later you

confessed it was a false alarm. You weren't going to be a father. How

can I not deduce that you, my little brother, competed with me on

every aspect of my life. Enough examples?

You had never given me one decent compliment on my

accomplishments which were many. Several friends called me gifted. I

blushed with the praise and said, no way. You were my baby brother

with issues of your own. I didn't want you to feel inferior or worthless,

lacking self-confidence. I shouldn't have bothered. Must have been in

the DNA you inherited from our father—an egomaniac, a scumbag just like him. Yes, you were the one who was like our father. Tikras Tevas. Mama was afraid of you so she always took your side. I hear you're writing plays also, another poetry book. Sėkmės. Good luck!

YOU: Louis Dudek and I conceived *Pluriel*—as well as the Ben's Poets Corner—during our eternal discussions throughout the 70s at Ben's deli. You weren't around then. But to encourage your literary and artistic talents, I let you do the posters for my series. I discovered the Cafe Commune as our permanent venue. I froze my butt off putting up most of the posters around Montreal. I didn't need, or ask for your support "financially and emotionally", cheap lunches at Harvey's. And I certainly didn't need your childish guilt trips about your pregnancy. I needed bilingual support, someone with a good head on her shoulders to help me with the difficult emcee chores and multicultural diplomacy. *"It had to be about him always."* No. It always had to be about Canadian and Quebec nationalism, Lithuanian independence and the fight for peace during the Cold War era.

ME: OH PULEEZE!!!! Always about you you you. No I wasn't around because I had a day job and worked in the theatre and took art classes at night at Sir George towards a BFA while you went to McGill full time on our mother's bank account and graduated to become a teacher, oh, excuse me, I mean a tenured professor. Both our mother and I gave you a hand and were relieved that you found a career that did not require hard physical labour.

Now where to begin? Here's my memory: It was 1980 and we came together after our father's death. You approached me and offered the dove of peace, as you called it, or was it the feather of peace, and I took it. You had just published your first poetry collection and I congratulated you and asked: *now what do you want to do next?* And so you told me about *Pluriel,* nothing about Dudek. Why shine the light away from yourself as though nobody else was important. You admitted to not knowing how or where to start. I offered my help as I had some experience organizing corporate events and booking venues for my plays. You could get the readers you said but you needed a place and there was no money. I suggested the basement of St. James United Church in downtown Montreal where I had just finished rehearsing my second play, *Mirror Mirror.* No cost to you. Seemed fine at the time. It was a start.

A young emerging poet, Michael Ondaatjee, was your first reader. I was not into poetry at that time and didn't give a sheep's shit who these people were. For me, everyone was created equal. The word status was never in my vocabulary. I designed the flyers (this was before computers) and posted them around the downtown core in rain, snow and sunshine because YOU asked me too. You never froze your butt!

Come see my scrapbook where I keep all the posters I created. I even wrote a couple of press releases when you were short on time. My assistance went beyond stapling flyers to telephone poles around the city or leaving notices at the library. The reading series later moved to an art gallery and then the Cafe Commune, which was the venue you discovered. I always give credit where credit is warranted. I was proud of you.

You never asked me for help with emcee duties or diplomacy, so stop fabricating what was never demanded of me. I just did what you asked. I guess it was never enough for you. Always about you. You never mentioned that you had talked to Dudek about your reading

series. You wanted me to believe it was all your idea. And if Pluriel
was concocted by both of you, why wasn't he there for the first night?

Unlike you, a shiftless unemployed pretentious poet, a
freeloader, I had a day job which I hated but I had financial obligations
to our mother and you to help with the rent and, if you weren't so
egotistical and ostentatious, you would know that Harvey's was all I
could afford on a secretary's salary. You were a taker, a low life again,
like our father. Never gave me or our mother anything but grief. But
she stuck by you because you scared her. *"Tikras Tievas. Like his
father",* she would say to me when you weren't around. Repeat so it
sticks glued to your soft brain, LIKE YOUR FATHER. I do recall
your acting the part of the impoverished poet stealing jam and peanut
butter sandwiches and pocketing them from literary events and parties.
Your melody of poverty always rang false. So sorry I couldn't afford
the Ritz.

As for Ben's Poets Corner, that too was your deal with Louis
Dudek. Knew nothing about it although I do recall your using a photo I
took of you which hung in the poet's corner next to Dudek's, with his

holding up a giant cucumber the size of his arm. So phallic. Big laugh.

It is from there that I realized poets were a different breed, or I should

preface that statement by saying that a lot of the poets I met at that

time were pretentious assholes.

You spoiled my initial love for poetry, or perhaps I let you, but

I also moved on. *"Use your other talents,"* friends and strangers

advised me. Being an introvert, I preferred my own company, writing

stories, sketching portraits, pursuing a creative life.

Not sure what you mean about childish guilt trip in my

pregnancy. I didn't realize a university education spawned such

ignorance, or is it just stupidity, sibling rivalry on your part again. That

would be 1985 and I was still designing your Pluriel flyers; still

plastering them around downtown Montreal until I could no longer

help you because I had developed complications in my pregnancy. As

a so-called sensitive educated poet, gestational diabetes is a serious

disease for both the baby and mother-to-be but, of course, your

concern was more about the birth of your reading series and getting

those damn posters up. So that last year, 1986, yes, you had to freeze your butt off putting them up yourself while the cops in hot pursuit followed behind and tore them off their posts. Now you know how that feels. I was ordered bed rest before my son was born, or you would have lost a sister and a nephew, but you didn't know the real world; only fantasyland.

You never inquired about my health or how I was doing overall. You showed no empathy for anyone but your own glorification and your place in the League of Poets, Lithuania's saviour. Perhaps they should raise you to sainthood. Even family never mattered. This behaviour of yours went unnoticed because you were my little brother and I understood your desperation in being recognized and that you suffered the same consequences I did growing up. My best friends and future husband revealed the corruption of all your emotions; how you used and abused me. The quiet wound again. If I retaliated, you poured more of your venom onto my spirit and left me in tatters. I no longer cry. All cried out.

So a multicultural reading series was about peace during the Cold War era and Lithuanian Independence. How is that going? I thought Pluriel was a great way to understand the diversity that is Canada. I give you credit for that but don't hail yourself as anything else. You are no icon, nobody's saviour. Certainly not to the people who know you best. I am a Canadian and do not relish looking back on the past. I am not its prisoner. My culture vaporized me; amnesia swallowed up the language, like a bottle of Vodka. Mother spoke to me in fractured English. My tongue lost the words, the patter, the lingo of our pagan ancestors.

YOU: Because you can't speak French, you were fired from your secretarial job. That's why you "moved to Alberta". Not because you "didn't want to rain on my parade". Your torrent of attacks also included my writer friends—or even the Centaur Theatre. Again to encourage your writing interests, I would get you free tickets that you would always pressure me for. Afterwards, again and again, you thanklessly attacked me and The Centaur. Every show!

ME: How presumptuous! You obviously have dementia or close to it. I suggest you investigate your shrinking memory cells. You do not know your sister so I will address your comments again. I was bilingual, so much so that I was considered for a promotion to our Communications Dept. I was NOT fired. That would have been my story to our mother because I didn't want to hurt her. After everything done to me, I still had a heart.

I knew it would be your turn to take care of her. It was a difficult decision to make but one I had to in order to salvage my sanity and provide a future for my son, have my husband see his elderly parents before they kicked off. He had remained in Montreal all those years out of respect for my wishes, and then in 1993, I had had enough of Quebec politics, your bullying tactics, your micromanaging my life, our mother's dysfunctional behaviour towards me especially in regard to what her husband, my so-called father had done to me. Jesu Jesu.

My company, like a lot of corporate head offices at that time, were downsizing after the 1976 election of the Parti Quebecois. They could no longer do business in a province with a separatist government that did not recognize the democratic rights and freedoms of all its citizens. I had worked for the same firm for 23 years and, since they were handing out packages, I took the opportunity and approached our Human Resources department asking for a severance pay. It would be a means for us to leave a province that was exploding from the inside out. Human Resources wanted me to stay and even offered me a promotion, more money, but I declined. I had to go, not only because of what was happening in Quebec, but the package would provide a means to start a new life in my husband's hometown, Edmonton, and get away from my "toxic" family.

Hubby always respected my wish to stay and he understood. He was surprised when I walked into the kitchen that day after work and said, *"it is time. I cannot live here anymore."* I also felt there was no future if I remained. I was 46. It was now or never, and I needed to escape all of you, needed to heal all my wounds. I knew it would be a hardship for you to take care of our mother. You had never been a caregiver. I can tell you it was the best decision I ever made.

As for the Centaur, not sure what you meant about attacks as it was normal to analyze a work of art and offer critiques as you had done with my work.

And finally, who attacked whom? I never spoke negatively of you or your work even when it was pretentious shit. For me, family was supposed to always be there for support. I learned that from neighbours who took me in as a child. I never asked you for Centaur tickets. I received a freebie now and again by an actor friend who knew the Artistic Director and had acted in some of the plays. Either you were experiencing an amnesiac moment, or you were searching for another stone to hurl at me. Emotional abuse is your way of controlling my life, or is it just for me you save your vile remarks. You never ever encouraged my writing. Yes, you didn't want me to rain on your parade. Instead, I clearly remember you suggesting I stick to painting since I had no other talent. Stop fabricating lies. Grow up.

YOU: You had married a bum from out West, a hulk with personal issues. You had met him at the YMCA where he was sleeping on the floor with other transients. The bum quickly began to beg for money from me and mama. *"The Bank of Bena"*. She generously gave you money for the first instalment on your house, as well as for your car, from her meagre savings as a cleaning lady. The bum continued to mooch money off mama all the while criticizing her cooking, lifestyle and European values. I was the only man standing between him and *"The Bank of Bena"*. This is why mama trusted me and excluded both of you from her will in 1986, as well as from her revised will in 2010.

Your selective memory failed to mention her will and her choice to protect her money. Mama was tired of supporting both of you, constantly biting the hand that fed you. A daughter in her 50s and her husband never weaned from the womb. Shame! She had become afraid of your "aggressive" ways. A daughter, a dagger. That's why she didn't want to see both of you in person any more. Mama and I had warned you not to marry that useless hulk, not *"because he wasn't Lithuanian"* but because we thought that you deserved someone better than a bum off the street.

We were right. That wimpy hulk turned out to be always sick, always unemployed, always going back to school and always stooping so low as to beg for money from his Christian mother-in-law, instead of borrowing from a local bank. Taking advantage of an old pensioner, how low can you go? That's what you did "wrong".

ME: Man? The measure of a man is how he treats his family. Baby brother YOU WERE NEVER A MAN. What an imagination! For some inexplicable reason you and our mother seemed to want to manipulate my life, a diversion tactic from your own miserable lives I guess. Again, come sit by me and bring your tiny brain with you. Shouldn't be difficult since it is lightweight, a balloon full of hot air. Let me relate this incident. Perhaps it'll shake up some of those useless cognitive cells. I will excuse onset of early dementia but; otherwise, you are a poor excuse for a human being.

The summer of 1971. I was 24 and you still a babe in our mother's arms at 21. So I forgive your lack of recollection. How little you know of me. My "bum" had left Edmonton like so many others from small town Canada and hitched across the country sleeping in Youth Hostels, converted barns, and rooms in the YWCA on Dorchester Street—transient idealistic young hippies, out to see the world. My future-to-be husband had no personal issues. You did. I have no idea where you got the idea that he asked our mother for money. He didn't know her. I provided money to both of you when I could barely afford my rent on Lorne Avenue. I admit when we married and had our son, our mother helped with a deposit on a car and house. That's what families do you told me years later when you requested money from me for our mother's care.

What I remember is that two of my best friends and the "bum" pointed out to me how you were both taking advantage of my generosity. I started making a secretary's salary and I was *The Bank of Dolly"* and kept slipping money into your pocket as did our mother. You played the poor hungry poet over and over while I paid your way so you wouldn't starve. You knew how to manipulate so well—a con man using others to get your way, just like our father.

Our mother squealed on you. Said she gave you $4,000 for alimony when you divorced your first wife who left you for someone with a full bank account. What you don't know, my dear baby brother, is that when we sold our house to move to Edmonton, we paid back what we owed her. Did you ever pay our mother back the money she ripped out of her RRSPs to pay your tuition to McGill and for your

divorce? Amazing the information you choose to leave out of your life

dossier so I look like the bad sister.

I learned that summer how love could hurt. My first big amour

ditched me for a girl of his own faith, and once again my heart was left

in tatters. I swore to him that I would convert, that we could have both

a Christmas tree and Hannukah candles for the holidays to show that

love has no fences. You and our mother were thrilled. He was a law

student at McGill, wealthy, from a prestigious family in Westmount. It

was always about money and prestige for both of you; a mother who

could live on a dime and you spending every dime she gave you on

yourself. You disgust me. But the law student ditched me, threw me

into the river like that rag doll you keep writing about.

Some of my theatre friends were volunteers at the Y and I

joined them in making these transients feel welcomed to Montreal,

assuring they had everything they needed before they went on to

explore the next province. It was the sixties; hippies filled the hostels,

the YWCA, and park benches in Dominion Square. I was buying

coffee for everyone at the Y. Kept me busy; kept me from reflecting

on how love is the greatest wound of all. I asked the "bum" who was

sitting on the floor if he wanted coffee. He looked up, smiled and

nodded his head. It was love at first sight on his part but not mine

because I now distrusted men (like our mother) and anyone who said

they loved me. I was still recuperating from the broken relationship

with the law student.

I wouldn't say criticize was the correct usage of the word. This

western "bum" was not familiar with European food or the Christian

lifestyle our mother routinely followed and expected everyone to

honour. Not sure I understand what you mean about European values.

Values are values and he valued honesty, integrity, generosity and

kindness, unlike you, my little brother, the wannabe phoney baloney

poet.

How dare you try to run my life! You had no right. I suppose it

gave you a sense of authority, power, to tell me whom I should or

shouldn't date as though you were my father. I understand your lack of role models. As an adult, you should have seen a counsellor to guide your way.

In 1990 we vacationed in Edmonton to escape the crisis that was always Montreal whether political or Indigenous. My husband fell off his younger brother's horse and broke his femur. I later found out it was intentional. Sibling rivalry has no restrictions, speaks the same language everywhere. He waited three years for a new hip. So no, he couldn't work and I took care of everyone and everything—cooking, cleaning, yard work, shopping, a husband on crutches/or in a wheelchair, and our five-year-old son who was a growing concern, about to start school. Every morning I woke up early to wait for the bus to take me across the Mercier Bridge into Montreal and work. We survived. Because what choice did we have? Life.

By 1993 I had had enough of your narcissistic superego and Quebec politics and so we moved to Edmonton where it was the *bum's* turn to be with his family. He told me to take a year off, to write; he now could get a job as a welder which he did, bad hip and knees. He worked the last few months for his journeyman welding ticket and received his Red Seal. He found a job easily in Edmonton. Had just started his new trade when the hip began to give him trouble and he needed further surgery to adjust the mistakes of the Montreal surgeons. A set back. He could no longer at the age of 45 do physical work so took a year to re-train in sales, learn to use a computer. A top student, No. 1 in his class, he received a scholarship. If it had happened to you, you would have run back crying to our mother.

As life has it, we were again getting back on our feet when he was diagnosed with stage 4 Colon Cancer. This *bum*, so strong in spirit, never complained. In your later life you will deal with your own cancer and perhaps that was foisted on you so you would develop an understanding of what it felt to not be able to provide for your family. If I ever see you again, I will smash your face into a thousand pieces like a Jurassic Park puzzle so you would know what real pain feels.

As I understand it, what you're telling me I did wrong was to marry a good man with values, not perfect, but one with a generous soul who lifted me in my darkest moments. Who the hell do you think you are? I never ever spoke ill of you or your desire to be a poet unlike our mother who would doublespeak and complain to me about you behind your back. Even you moved out a couple of blocks away from her in Verdun while attending university because you couldn't stand her and yet you speak with a crooked mouth, pronouncing her a saint, strong like prayer book leather you said while taking her money and never paying back.

What did I do wrong? I was born in a family of liars who felt a need to abuse me in various forms: emotionally bringing me to my knees when I did nothing wrong. Physically and sexually, because I was born a girl and girls can take that kind of treatment. I was a good girl. Many others with lesser complaints and mental issues become suicidal. I was a survivor and none of you could ever destroy me try as you might.

YOU: Yes, you did phone mama "every Sunday" from Edmonton, too often to ask for more money! And when mama would enquire about what you were going to do with her sent money, you would abusively reply: None of your business.

ME: Little brother, you have it all backwards. If she sent any money it was for her grandson to buy a gift for him for his birthday, Christmas or just because, *"he vants a bike. I send money"*. SHE was the one who in the year before she jumped out her second floor window asked me for money. She always wanted $250 which I figured was her rent money. I sent her $500 a couple of times and, again, she would insist that she only needed $250.

You, big shot, who wiped your ass with dollar bills, didn't even know she was in need because you stayed away, had nothing to do with her, never saw her. If I ever asked her for money from Edmonton, it would have been because we had none and about to go on welfare. Happened once in between jobs and never happened again. Pride got in my way so I didn't tell her and a month later I found a job and paid her back. So get your head screwed straight so your brain can function, and tell the truth. Tikras Tievas, you creep. His likeness is yours. Repeat this mantra until it sinks into your head.

YOU: It's a total lie that I "rarely visited" mama. I had to take care of her cataract operation. I accompanied her to doctors' appointments. I spent every weekend for over a year leafing through a 138 page CLSC booklet, checking out nursing homes, public and private. We communicated every day. Mama suffocated me with calls. She even called me once on my cell while I was teaching in the classroom! I visit her every Friday now at her nursing home. MAMA NEVER EVER SPEAKS ABOUT HER DAUGHTER. (You knew this while you were writing to straighten out the "record.") Why does your own mother never ever mention you? Because of your senior abuse.

ME: Wow! Let's put this in the proper context. First of all, you couldn't live with her when you were a McGill student and moved a few blocks down in Verdun. It was easier for you to get a handout, living the life of a poor poet instead of saving some money and this time helping our mother with expenses as I always did. Of course, baby, you had to take care of her AFTER I moved to Edmonton. That's why it took me so long to make a decision about leaving Montreal. I could have gone earlier but stayed the course because I wasn't sure about your emotional stability to take care of anyone especially our mother.

Such dominance you held over her; she told me she was afraid of you. Tikras Tievas. Games played out and no one won. She didn't want to come with me to Edmonton. She wanted to be close to her church and you. She had no choice. I left and yep, it was your turn to help. Hard wasn't it? She's told me millions of times how she loved me but yep never ever spoke to you about me because she was afraid of your temperament. That's what she said; afraid all men were like the creep she married.

You had her under your wings. I was gone so she had no one but you to rely on now even if it was through fear of your ill-treatment towards her. We took her for Sunday drives in the country; I had lunch with her downtown. Smago* she would say. She told me she enjoyed our time together and in those quiet moments she complained about you and that you were just like our father. Always that. In some ways she played us against each other. We'd have her over for dinner and visited every Sunday. She relished her pupuluka, (an endearment for her grandson), which you totally ignored because that was another thing you couldn't have. She doted on him your nephew, whom you also ignored. He never did anything to you except be my beautiful son.

121

Jealousy reared its ugly head again. Why couldn't you just all be happy for me?

Senior abuse? I've heard you yell and scream at our mother as loud as your crooked mouth would carry; taken money to cover your alimony, living expenses. Go take a memory pill and be gone. And, yes, in her final years, you told me what a nuisance she was, always calling you for something or other, interrupting your class while teaching. You preferred relying on the bank and social services of Dolly and Bena Inc. Scum! If I follow your reasoning: Did YOU ever pay back the money you owed her?

YOU: After mama's accidental fall, (due to improper medication, it has been established now), you didn't want to come and comfort her. You jabbered on the phone longer about your dead dog than about your mother in the emergency ward! So my Filipino wife suggested that you *"send money for her care"* because that is the tradition in the Phillippines when a family member can't attend to an emergency. But typical PIS projection, you tried to make me, a tenured teacher, look like the mooch! Funny how selective memory can remember this one isolated request—from my wife and not from me. Yet, you totally

blocked out your decades of demands for cash from the *"The Bank of*

Bena" to pay off your endless debts...followed by your endless

ingratitude and endless snipes at your generous mother.

ME: What a hypocrite you are. Funny how I was a mooch asking my

family for help in a family emergency when my husband broke his hip

and then suffered through stage 4 colon cancer and I had a house and

family to take care of. It was always about money where you were

concerned. All for you. What kind of man are you? We've been

through this diatribe a hundred times and won't repeat it as you, the

educated tenured professor, obviously can't seem to understand what

YOU did.

 And she did not fall accidentally. The year before, our calls

ended with mama warning me that if I called her and there was no

answer, to call you. Does that sound like an accidental fall? Then one

Sunday there was no answer and so I called you as per our mother's

request. Your wife's sister, I believe, answered and told me our mother

had jumped out the window from her second floor flat and you and what's her face, the Goddess from the Sea, were at the hospital. Your

wife's sister sounded frightened. Said she wasn't allowed to talk to

me. Can I assume she feared you and your physical and mental abuse?

Doesn't sound like an accident to me although that is what you would

like to believe to assuage your guilt and put the blame on me as you

always conveniently did.

I do recall you asking me for money, $1,000, for her care.

"Instead of taking a plane back to Montreal, send money." Your usual

tripe. I was concerned the money would not go to our mother but into

your own pocket for the reno work on your house so I demurred. I

didn't trust you as our mother never trusted you. I was here and you

remained in Montreal calling me a non-Canadian because I had left.

Which one was I? A non-Canadian or a non-Lithuanian?

As for any inheritance, whenever mentioned, I would tell our

mother to keep her money for herself, to spend it on what gave her

pleasure. I never cared about money. I was never a material girl. I was

a hippie chick. All I required was peace and love and giving life a

chance. I wished for a family who loved me. I guess it wasn't in you to know what real love was. You were never taught so how would you know? Our mother and I always ended our calls with I love you and she asked me not to talk to you because she was afraid you would harm her. Senior abuse? You effing idiot. I will repeat: she was afraid of you and YOUR senior abuse towards her.

I've kept our messages and correspondence so everything I've said here is saved and backed up because I knew one day I would have to defend myself against you and your lies. There were two predators in my childhood—you were the other. I have forgiven my mother for neglecting me because she didn't know any better.

So being a tenured professor makes you a big shot. YOU are the leech going all the way back when I bought you hot dogs because that was all I could afford and you talked against our generous mother to me. As for PIS. Didn't know what that was and had to look it up because when someone like a tenured professor starts throwing barbs at me with three letters of the alphabet, I need to understand their meaning. May I remind you again and again that whatever money we owed our mother, families do help families in a financial crisis, as your

Phillipina wife had stated. We paid back everything and more when we sold the house. I sent her rent money when I moved out here to start a new life with my husband and son. File that in your memory cells.

What more do you want me to say? And you? It broke our mother's heart when you changed faculties, and said you wanted to be a poet instead. She told me she didn't understand what a poet did. *"What that, poet?"* she would ask. So stop writing your life and your relationship to our mother and me as fiction. I suggest you see a therapist, you pretentious egotistical excuse for a human being. Do I sound angry?

YOU: And last but not least, my indelible memories of you are of a big sister, a bitter sneer. You inherited papa's facial resemblance, as well as his aggressive temperament. Two-faced, just like him, you know how to put on a polite front in public to make yourself look good. In private, just like him, you started the "incommunicado" standoff. It began in the 1970s when you were living in the McGill

126

ghetto with that bum, both of you constantly necking in front of me. I nevertheless tried to resolve our family feud. Feeling threatened, the hulk assaulted me. As I got up off the floor in the hallway, the words from your gritted teeth still ring in my ears today: *"Stay out of my life."* And that's exactly what mama and I have tried to do because of a sister and daughter suffering from PIS consenting to violence and abuse, while stubbornly living in a state of denial.

ME: Seemed to me you are talking about yourself and not me. But that is nothing new, my little ungrateful, lying brother. Let me try to refresh your memory cells again, which are based on my notes. First of all, I have always been told I look like our mother. She loved it when strangers asked if we were sisters. I have found early photos of our father in Germany and you resemble him. Sneer, albeit a crooked one but still a sneer. That was you.

Aggressive temperament. Yes, we all had that at one time or another to deal with our violent abusive household. Tragedy? The biggest tragedy is what trauma in the family does to relationships between the kids as they grow up. They go through something together, but after they become adults, they can't talk to each other. Instead of making them come together, trauma pushes them apart. When there's nothing to turn against, people end up taking out their anger on each other. After I moved you and our mother out of that house on Evelyn Street, I thought that we could at last be a family but no. You turned on me. Out of jealousy? Out of habit? I don't know. Our mother holds some responsibility. Love one another she would tell me. I asked her why you hated me and her response was: *"I don't know"* or *"forget the past."*

It is you who was unwilling to communicate. How quickly you forget. Sit here by my side baby brother again while I try once more to remind you. Living on Brown Blvd. Now, just the three of us, our anger towards each other went like this: I want to watch the Ed Sullivan show; no, I want to watch hockey; no, no no and you always got your way and so we watched hockey most of the time. Petty arguments, so juvenile now. When I turned 21, the legal age, I left like a displaced person to save my mental health and have some semblance of a happy human being. I was always an Honours student, didn't date, drink, do drugs. Just went to church every Sunday with you and our

128

mother, took photos of you both along the way as though we required a passport for entry to the gates of heaven. Our mother always made me wear tight fitting sheaths. She saw a "mini-her" in me and I was so sheltered, naive. Didn't see.

You both lost control over me when I left and you judged a man I loved and who loved me unconditionally, by your own prejudices. Call yourselves the Catholic hypocrites or pious flaw flaws as Sister Saint Mary Ronald called us in grade 5. I never ever told you how to live, whom to see, what to be but always encouraged you to be your best because if I criticized, you would read something unintended into my remarks.

So I hope, tenured teacher, that academia did not screw up your intelligence what little there was of it. Your behaviour towards me hurt our mother. You were both so nice to each other when you were kids she would say. But then I wasn't the monster. It was our father. There was always supposed to be a monster in our family. To appease our mother, twice, I repeat TWICE I presented you with the olive branch of peace and you said NO, YOU DIDN'T WANT TO SEE ME. So tell me again, who was the one who started this estrangement. Fuckin' liar.

You tried to resolve our family drama in your nightmares. Don't paint

yourself a hero because you never were. And I do recall telling you to

"stay out of my life" because I could no longer withstand the mental

and emotional abuse heaped on me by a demented brother who himself

needed help. I really don't understand why you constantly bring up

your favourite letters of the alphabet PIS. We were estranged but, as

you know, our mother and I always stayed in touch and feared you to

the end. Maybe you didn't know but now you do. Tikras Tievas she

would call you. Oh, did she say that about me too? How convenient.

The hulk indeed assaulted you on the way out of Algonguin

Park. You said you were penniless and needed a vacation so we

invited you to join us camping and to look for the Tom Thomson

grave. You were heading out to Toronto afterwards. You never offered

to pay for anything, not even gas. And so that day as we were heading

out of the park, we had to stop and suddenly in front of our faces you

were waving a wad of money for your trip to Toronto, counting fifty

dollar bills no less. You laughed in our faces with that devious smirk

of our father. Fooled us again. My hubby got so angry he threw you

130

out of the car like trash and wanted to drive away. He had had enough

of YOUR being the moocher. Indeed, other friends tried to warn me

about you but I refused to believe my little brother could be such a

selfish egomaniacal trickster. If you remember I told hubby to forget it

and to just drop you in Toronto. I still cared about you. I, even then,

defended you so don't bullshit me about your trying to save our

family. My friends saw the kind of something (not human) you were

and tried to warn me. I should have listened.

YOU: So my dear sister, you are obviously the one who needs

"therapy". You still have not *"broken the cycle"*. You still lack the

humour and the grace that shows genuine conquest of inner demons.

Instead, the papa in you, the PIS in you, is evident throughout.

ME: You wish. As of this interview, we have been estranged 25 years

so you, dear fuck up, still don't know your sister. You've invented a

fictionalized character for your next poem, insisting you were the

victim. Always so focused on your short arm and crooked Raymond

Massey smile. Strangers were easy to win over because you painted me as the evil one in our family's life and it was just the reverse. I believed you and our parents when they said I was no good, that I was a show girl because I pursued a career in theatre. The arts saved my life. I broke the cycle when I left home, read books to understand what had happened to me because I was so naive and in fear of you all.

That horrid night, our mother was awakened by the sound of pleasure and she opened her bedroom door to see my father violating my 13 year old body. I wept because I didn't understand what was being done to me. I was bleeding and thought I had harmed myself. Our mother kept up her facade with her usual jesu jesu, while she threw a Kotex pad at my face and I just kept crying *"I won't do it again, I won't do it again"*. I thought our father's assault was my fault. Life went on the next day...

If you find my grade 8 class photo, you will see the pain in my face. My marks that year plummeted. I was always an honours student. I started to write in a diary to understand what had happened to me but, of course, you wouldn't remember that. Dead memory cells. A mother in denial and a brother's abusive arrogant rivalry towards a sister he never knew but used. For the longest time, I blamed myself as most victims of any type of abuse directed towards them do. I learned from books, and friends who told me it was not my fault. Neighbours took me in when I had nowhere to go and fed my ego with self-worth and my body with food to sustain me.

I know you hate to hear this but baby brother, I am so blessed that as I write this last chapter of my life, I have a family who loves me, two grandsons and friends who continue to encourage and support me in every stage of my being. They tell me I have talent and to forget you and your tyrannical behaviour. They know the real you—the one that shows the crooked smile. Am I being cruel? You taught me how.

My anger will never disappear. I rage against the slurs and insults heaped on me as a child, for a mother that never protected me, for believing I was worthless, untalented, stupid. It's been a long journey and hope you have found some peace in your life among a household of foreign women whose culture begs to be submissive. Just your style. You can control them.

I spoke to our mother in the hospital shortly after her suicide attempt. She was a bit confused as I usually called her on a Sunday and that day it was Saturday. She was eating. I could hear the chomp of her meal between her words. She kept repeating: I love you, Dali, I love you. And I repeated, I love you, ma, I love you.

*Smagu—fun

CUDDA SHUDDA (for my brother)

i moonwalked

         the periphery of you

         ignoring spiteful slurs,

your spotlight, an illusion in your minim mind.

tearless eyes, disfigured smile, shrunken arm,

a botched up job in a DP camp. i saw only you,

my little brother whole with talent; overlooked the

sibling wars, the fragile ego hanging on a clothesline

         in a summer storm

         waiting for the rain to stop.

you beatified yourself a saint,

a legend in your own right, a narcissistic poet

searching for your star of fame

somewhere on the sidewalks of your brain.

         i no longer walk on eggshells

         my wounds have disappeared;

only scars remain; yours still percolate with hate.

we cudda been a family. cudda been so many things.

wasn't in your DNA—

cudda, shudda, you laughed as you walked away.

STANISLAUS

As I prepare for Ireland, I am reading Edna O'Brien's little book on James Joyce. This morning I just read a bit about James's relationship with his younger brother Stanislaus. It rang true to what you once wrote about your brother. Stanislaus looked up to Joyce but was jealous and competitive with him. Of course, Stanlislaus wasn't anywhere near the talented writer, but he was obsessed with trying everything that Joyce tried—mimicking him became a preoccupation — as did criticizing James for abandoning the family. (Stanislaus' diaries are focused on James). It seems that your brother was in the same position. And, I think that is the grievance that the younger sibling has toward the older one—the older one is usually the first person to "escape" the family and the remainders feel abandoned and betrayed. That feeling of ownership and prerogative of interpreting the family is what they hold onto.

...Jane, your best friend forever

LIETUVOS HIMNAS: THE NATIONAL ANTHEM OF LITHUANIA

i have assimilated—

blended with the mall mob; forgotten my pagan ancestry,

deleted the child i used to be shyly singing

in the church basement *Lietuva, Tėvyne mūsų** .

upstairs, followers worshipped at the altar of our Lady

Gate of Dawn, remembered the Hill of Crosses,

remembered Sauliai, my mother's birthplace

where her father carved, rebuilt roadside shrines

after their destruction. devout pilgrims came to pray.

Lietuva, i met you once—

sang about the forests carpeting the land, meekly

whispered while the others belted out their pride

so you could hear your native song, Tautiska Giesme.

i fiddled with the hem of my red dress, revealing a white slip;

eyes averted to your flag at attention—the yellow, green and red.

i am a confusion of languages—

English, Lithuanian, a mix of German, Latin, bad French.

i am an injured mutt, abused, abandoned, tied by the highway.

Lietuva, the land of heroes, i met you once, once in a dream

but i no longer chant your songs; no longer pray your mournful

runes, no longer speak your native tongue. forgotten one another.

in 1990 you won your independence; in 1968 i found mine.

i am a Canadian.

*Lietuva, Tėvyne mūsų — Lithuania, our fatherland

WISDOM OF THE WOLVES

I think I could turn, and live with animals,

They are so placid and self-contain'd,

I stand and look at them long and long

                        ...Leaves of Grass, Walt Whitman

                        some days—

i want to live in the woods among the wolves.

at least you know where you stand.

                        their needs are small—

water, food and they are on their way.

they don't require stroking or poking

these wild dogs. they run in packs,

three at the head: the aged, sick, set the pace

never left behind. the next five are the strongest

and the best, protect the front line. the middle infantry

soldier on against the foe. the remaining five

have everybody's back. the lone last one is leader

ensuring no one's left behind. keeps the pack on track.

always on point he herds in all directions; protects the family.

                                    wolves care for their own—

ask for nothing more. they do not whine or pine, or complain.

they do not scare. just howl; announce their presence.

seem so happy with so little, safe against the perils of the night.

i would sit on my front porch, and listen long and hard, long

and hard.

never tire of their wise refrains.

MAITINTOJO: SURVIVOR

brother said i was a no-talent freeloader,

such evil from a younger sibling.

your fault wiggling in the mirror,

you asked for it. your fault.

i had shimmied to the Beatles'

Twist and Shout. a turn-on for this teenage boy.

and always lobing PIS at me the few times

we connected. what was that? plot induced stupidity?

personal information system? ah, post incest syndrome.

had to look it up. you, you with the gargantuan ego,

dragging me into your neolithic youth.

you, you write your own story. i'll write mine. a deal?

i persevered your taunts and here i am. a survivor

retreating into writing poems, painting landscapes,

reading self-help books to understand my mangled years;

what had happened to me; why i was unloved. i let your

pretensions overtake my self-doubts; i loved you anyway.

no worry about you my mother said,

you be okay but your brother need me.

      her darling pet. guilt will do that every time.

i needed her more. she could provide the physical means

a family required, where my father couldn't—

food, a roof, schooling, clothing. love?

just a four-letter word. love

just a four-word sentence: *i have no time.*

and she had none to give. i understood but still

a daughter is a daughter she would say

when needful of help or money.

in her son's presence she would turn on me.

      right after Jesu, Jesu, Jesu.

HAPPINESS

carries no scars. it appears in small doses,

disappears without much notice.

sadness persists. tumours in remission,

announce themselves quietly—

until the next bout.

sadness is tenacious. velcro to the heart—

strenuous, arduous; difficult to dismiss.

happiness is fugacious; a temporary reprieve—

so watch your back.

THE LAST POEM

lying in a hammock

arms outstretched, five feet high and wide,

indigo fingers ink the moody sky.

chubby clouds

conceal the sun, red-like flames gone viral

parch and scorch the earth with fire,

barren; withered; shrivelled to a seed,

sick with fever, smog, contaminants

contained in a viral death.

watch the overflow of wasted water,

hungry rats running freely; eat their young,

vanished birds in empty skies. it has come to that.

next chance.

rebuild the broken cosmos, paint it flat,

sweep away the toxic mortals; start anew.

carry care for wounded daughters;

so only kindness will remain,

and the world will be at peace. I swear.

EPILOGUE: DOING THE RIGHT THING

*Stop thinking about what might have been if you hadn't left. You did
and you did the right thing. Hell, you're letting your mother put you on
a guilt trip without even talking to her. Stop it!*
...Gayle, childhood friend, July 2007

The Quiet Wound ends with my leaving home at the age of 21—
that was the legal age in Quebec at that time and no one, neither my
mother nor brother could hold me back. My parents were already
divorced.

Author, Flannery O'Connor, has stated that anybody who survived
their childhood would carry enough information with them to last the
rest of their days. Notwithstanding the physical and sexual abuse,
insults, curses, accusations, criticisms and violence that defined my
childhood, producing an unhappy adult, I survived. That door to the
encoded memories can be opened and we can persevere under a united
front. Trauma remains like a tumour in remission, rears its ugly head
when confronted. The molestation and other violations done to me did

indeed alter my personality in that I developed strength of character and an instinct for self-preservation. And always that rage that has now become ingrained in my consciousness as a coping mechanism, a shield against all wounds, mistrust in humanity. Sitting on that grey enclosed back porch on Evelyn Street, I would write and cry with the wolves until my tears dried up like an empty vessel.

It was the #MeToo movement that compelled me to cautiously raise my arms high in solidarity and admit that I too had been violated—physically, sexually and emotionally. It was the first step. Because of mobility problems, I could only join the protests in spirit and wore my pussycat hat in comradeship. These marches were blatant because women had to fight to be believed, to be heard. Many remained silent out of fear especially when they experienced emotional abuse, which is the more difficult to prove—my word against his, no other evidence. The quiet wound felt less quiet when my poetry, essays, plays, and artwork were spoken through a loudspeaker.

There are those who would side with my parents and excuse their behaviour by reminding me that they had endured hardships and disturbing events in their youth outrunning the bombs that exploded around them as they zig-zagged towards safety. They carried back painful images to their new home in Montreal, Quebec, Canada. And yet I have met other immigrants, family acquaintances with similar backgrounds who were determined to provide a better life for themselves and their families. Jonas Mekas, a Lithuanian author, and filmmaker, says in his book, *I Had Nowhere to Go,* that for immigrants, it is an infernal adjustment.

As for my brother, he had his own demons to overcome, and I was easy prey, the big sister.

My healing began

A. by admitting what had happened to me wasn't my fault. I was just a child and obeyed an adult, an authority figure.

B. by seeing the words on paper—molestation, abuse, violence—shouting the words.

C. by researching psychological and self-help books to understand my continuous ingrained anger which followed me into adulthood.

D. by writing this book so that others in similar circumstances could find solace in knowing they were not alone, not at fault and, therefore, could break the cycle that so often remained in families from one generation to the next.

E. by sending The Quiet Wound into the world. This has taken courage—and a glass of wine.

For my mental well-being, I eventually abandoned my family; fled Montreal to live in Edmonton, Alberta. Many might scold me especially the babushkas* in the Lithuanian community because a daughter just doesn't leave. Family is family. I've deleted my brother from my world as he has deleted me from his. Today, as of this writing, we have been estranged for thirty years. We had connected a few times in an effort to negotiate a peace treaty but it was not to be. No sooner did I forgive him, when everything repeated itself. People do not change; he had not changed and continued to drag me down to his antiquated youth.

We make our lives what we want it to be by the decisions we make, which are based on our values. I value family, books, writing, painting and a day overflowing with love and joy and sunshine. While life has its drama, I try to remember that, although happiness may come in small doses, accept the moment for what it is and then move on. Why waste time in an unsolvable situation. Live deliberately as Thoreau has been quoted.

I've outgrown the trauma of a lost childhood and youth but continue to deal with the existing rage, which some days can be overwhelming. It hasn't left me yet—it's now ingrained, shaped by those experiences. I try to avoid toxic people by using a different path on my journey. If I walk among poison ivy, I will get infected. I am determined to take another route. And so should you. Mobilize and raise your voice.

*babushkas – an old woman/grandmother

If you as a human being need help in an abusive situation, here are the numbers for the National Domestic Abuse Hotline:

Call: 1-800-799 SAFE (7233)

TTY: 1-800-787-3224

TEXT: "START" to 8878

If you as a human being need to report domestic violence, call your local police or 9-1-1

ACKNOWLEDGEMENT: THIS BOOK IS FOR

—all the immigrant women

lost in an assembly line of broken dreams

who still keep hoping for a better life.

—all the violated women

abused emotionally, physically, sexually

who leave behind a shattered life.

—all the silenced women

scared to voice their thoughts

who find their tongue and speak out loud.

—all the plain women

scorned in love, dismissed in life

who find beauty in their luminosity.

—all the strong women

perennials who keep bouncing back

no matter what life throws at them.

— all the brave women

who have had ENUF.

this book is for you.

ABOUT THE AUTHOR

Dolly Dennis is a multifaceted published author of two novels. The Quiet Wound is her first non-fiction book. Her work has appeared on stage, in literary journals, newspapers, anthologies, and the CBC. In Montreal, her first play, *The Plexiglass Box,* won two awards at the Quebec Drama festival. Shortly after moving to Edmonton in 1993, her short stories began to appear in several literary journals. In 2012 she was nominated for an Alberta Literary award for short creative non-fiction. She was one of the founders and organizers of the Glass Door Coffeehouse Reading series and is currently a member of the Writers Guild of Alberta and the Writers Union of Canada. Although writing is her first love, Dolly is also a visual artist whose paintings have been exhibited and sold to private collectors. She studied under Phillip Surrey at Sir George Williams (Concordia University) in Montreal. She is currently working on her fourth book, a short story collection.

This book was independently published by Jane Hikel. For more information, please contact: JaneHikel@yahoo.com

www.ingramcontent.com/pod-product-compliance
Lightning Source LLC
Chambersburg PA
CBHW070932130626
46555CB00001B/396